I0505078

Table of contents (TOC)

Chapter 1: Imagine yourself being successful

The Universal Law Of Attraction

The Universal Law of Attraction holds that thoughts, if held long enough, become tangible things. As such, those who dwell on dark thoughts end up realizing dismal results. Although the veracity of this law is universally challenged, it is in equal measure ubiquitously practiced and accepted. After a thorough debate, it has been concluded that the universal law of attraction works for those who believe it works and not to work for those who think it does not work. What you believe is what you get.

Read on to discover to know why you should imagine yourself being successful.

See Yourself As A Victor – Not A Victim

Therefore, it is the high time you stopped seeing yourself as a victim and instead started seeing yourself as the victor. You can be a loser if you decide that you are already one. Never imagine yourself failing because you soon will start to fail. Instead, imagine yourself being successful and you soon will. Thoughts become tangible things. Mix your thoughts with words and faith and compress the three together until they bear fruits.

Talk Yourself To The Very Pinnacle OF Success

Talking oneself to success is one trick that the greatest achievers have perfected. Instead of demeaning yourself through your own thoughts, you should take the unsullied chance and elevate yourself in the mind. Words that you speak have a profound effect on you. When in a tough situation, talk positively to yourself. For instance, you may utter: "the darkest hour is closest to dawn, hardships don't last forever – I soon will be out of this situation." Such positive words are good food to the soul. Note that negative utterances have a reverse effect on you! Never say anything negative about yourself. As you talk positive things, you soon begin thinking positive thoughts as well, and thoughts become things!

Acquire A Positive Attitude

An illustration is always given of two young men who were shortlisted for some crucial interview. One had a very negative attitude toward anything in life, a pessimist in another language. The other was a painstaking optimist who saw the best part of all things. As such, they took a different path as they waited for the interview. The optimistic fellow toured the interview hall in advance and began his rehearsals before an imaginary panel of interviewers. He could even imagine himself receiving motivating feedback from the panelists and finally clinching the position. The pessimist kept fearing the approach of the interview day until it finally was interview time and presented himself ill-confident and shy and failed the interview – just like he had anticipated!

Conclusion - Success Begins In The Mind

Success begins in the mind. Imagine your success and achieve it in the mind way before you strive to achieve it in real life! Those who succeed choose to succeed. It can also be said that those who fail often think themselves as failures and thus accept and endorse their situation. After all, who do you think achievers are? They are just failures who refuse to accept their present situation and strive to change it for the better. They must begin by speaking against their present circumstances in order to motivate positive thoughts. Once they have acquired a mental status that coincides with their positive utterances, they start imagining themselves being successful. And they indeed become successful! That simple!

Chapter 2: Make a timeline of what you want to achieve

For you to be successful in what you want to achieve, you must work using a timeline. It is good to have a timeline in your thoughts. However, it is more effective to have the same on paper. You can do this successfully by taking the following steps:

Take an A4 size sheet of paper and fold it in half using the horizontal axis. If you can only get standard paper, turn it so as to use it in the landscape format.

Along the horizontal axis, draw a horizontal line to signify the positive events that you associate with pleasure, place a + sign on the top right corner, above the horizontal axis place a negative sign on the bottom right corner below the horizontal axis.

It will be used to represent any events on your timeline that are associated with stress or displeasure. Decide whether to put every event on your chronological list whether below or above the horizontal axis on your timeline by marking every single one with a "-" or "+" sign. For each of your key events, represent them by drawing a dot on the horizontal; axis of your timeline.

Make sure there is ample space between events to allow them being spread across the axis from left to right end points. Draw a line for each event from each dot (either below or above the horizontal line). Based on its assigned numeric value, make the line as short or tall as its intensity.

This is the same as about a third of an inch for each interval on the scale. This means that a length of a line assigned 5 as intensity should be the same as 1 2/3 inches. Allow for sufficient space since recording one event may lead to the trigger of another memory. The points you have marked should be connected up. Remain open in adding events as you finish the timeline. It is natural for a single event to trigger the memory of one or several more events.

Whether you believe it or not, your life's story will be rich with meaning. It is also a useful way to capture such meanings which is similar to having your entire life in a snapshot. One of the innate emotional drives is seeking meaningful connections in life. It is connected to language, another ability that is unique to human beings. In many different ways, life is a process of telling your story while filling in any details as you go along, reinterpreting and interpreting meanings.

In addition to capturing such meanings, the exercise is an opportunity to examine a few things. According to yourself, you can examine things such as your wants, passions, needs, emotions, thoughts, past, life and so on. It is however challenging and courageous to liberate your mind from old stories and make sure you stand in the truth of your highest aspirations. Making a timeline is not only good for helping you achieve your objectives and goals, but it will also help you have a better understanding of yourself and your personality.

Chapter 3: Follow your intuition

Importance

Have you ever had a hit of knowing something to be true without knowing why? Have you ever had the gut feeling that you need to do something without having the explanation why you need to do it? And when you did the thing you were quite glad you listened to your sixth sense and did it? This so called feeling or gut feeling is actually our intuition. Each one of us has it, but only a few of us use it.

Why do few people use it? In any business studies, you will be told to look at the data before you make any decisions. Even though this is sound advice, it is only halfway helpful. The combination of rational mind and intuition is what distinguishes great business leaders from the good ones. We are rewarded every time we tap into our intuition. It is the messages that we get, sometimes they may feel like nudges, which will bring us down the path of success.

If this resonates with you, you will be ready to have a look at the importance of intuition. The importance will show you why following your intuition will result in personal, business and professional success. Furthermore, there are many benefits associated with following your intuition. In fact, there are no disadvantages that can be noted which are the result of following your gut.

Identification

One of the most important points of using your intuition is identifying your true sense of purpose and mission. You will be moved faster to your definition of success by following your dreams while being clear in what you want in life. Your intuition can be described as the compass that will ensure you achieve your objectives faster and effectively.

Ideas

Listening to your intuition helps you become open to new ideas which your rational mind may not be open to. Paying attention to your intuition will put an end to limiting patterns the rational mind may not be open to. It will also put an end to the limiting patterns provided by your rational mind, which will result in missed opportunities. Your intuition will ultimately help you see new things as " ideas " you otherwise would not be able to see or understand.

Sense

Your intuition is the only thing that can help you know when things are not quite right. This can either be in your work or personal relationships. Sensing this is important as it will allow you tweak your tactics or approach based on how others are behaving instead of based on what they are saying. When dealing with people, especially in business, it is critical as it can break or make a successful relationship or deal.

Caution

The voice of caution can only be heard by using your intuition. Following your gut or sixth sense when it tells you to steer clear of something is priceless. Understanding risk is vital to any business. Your intuition is, therefore, important as it is the only thing that can give you caution when in any business or personal relationship.

Chapter 4: Take risks wisely

Risk taking is required in the uncertain, fast-changing environment that forms our existence. One individual stated that you cannot wait for all stoplights to turn green if you are traveling from New York City to Los Angeles.

In business, the majority of people who fail are those that do not take risks. They fail to note that risks are taken every day in different facets of their lives. For example, risks are faced when they make choices about relationships they establish, what they eat for lunch and routes they take to and from work. So why is it that risk taking in business is more challenging? Usually, it is because the uncertainties loom larger. On the other hand, it may be that the person may not have experience to navigate and calibrate the risks. The following are some strategies that can be implemented to ensure risk taking is more palatable:

Being clear about hopes

Pursue only the things that really make sense to what your objectives and goals are as well as what you want to do. The majority of individuals veer off course by pursuing current trends or what looks hot'. In some cases, risk aversion can be a voice (our intuition) helping us avoid anything that is not right for us business-wise or personally.

Visual map development

You can come up with a results chain that describes the sequence of circumstances or events essential to achieving your goals and objectives. Drawing a picture will assist you communicate and visualize the risks. The same picture can be shared with others who can assist you assess the accuracy of your understanding. Sharing with others will also let them share their experience in dealing with similar risks.

Commitments and resources should be triggered as the risks resolve

Venture investors, some of the highest and most acclaimed risk takers, actually manage risks quite aggressively. For further investment, they target milestones. Such a move ensures focus is maintained. It also prevents betting the farm' before you have ploughed the ground.

Having more than one choice

Everything looks white or black if you do not have choices. This means that you will not have any flexibility to adapt to changes. Contingency plans and choices are required to support risk taking as they offer ways to adjust and recover.

In life, you can only take risks wisely after you have done an assessment of the risk involved. For example, if you want to take a shortcut to work to avoid traffic, you will want to choose the best shortcut. In some cases, you may need the fastest way despite the risks involved. In such cases, the wear and tear of the vehicle, risk of getting into an accident or risk of being fined are all less than the risk of losing the job or contract you are rushing to. In such a scenario, taking the shortcut is a wise risk as it guarantees future financial stability despite the chances of incurring additional expenses.

Chapter 5: Focus on your main objectives

When we are trying to work on our main objectives, focus is what keeps us on track. Think of an archer as they aim a target. S/he may only hit the bull's eye if they focus. Similarly, when you want to create something in your life, you must focus in order to achieve the objective. The following are some tips that will assist you stay focused on your objectives.

Write the objectives down: put your beliefs, objectives, reasons and goals in writing. When they are in writing, they are more realistic and they can be used as a source of encouragement and reviewed from time to time. Eventually, the main objective will become branded in your mind.

Minimize distractions: get rid of any temptation that deviates you from achieving your objective. If you plan on losing weight, get rid of any delivery and takeaway food menus that you get through your mail box. If your objective is spending money and reducing expenditure, you should unsubscribe from any services that are not necessary. Avoid subscriptions to text alerts, email, promotional newsletters, gaming and shopping. For instance, if your objective is to increase your exercise routing and you find the television to be a distraction, it should not be switched on until you have achieved your goal. You will be able to focus only by using every method you can think of to remove distractions.

Power of visualization: if we are to focus on something properly, we need to have a strong visual picture of our target. This is the only way to maintain focus on the end result. You will be able to give your objective more focus the more you bring it to the forefront of your mind.

Progress measurement: analyzing your progress is the only way you can control your progress. Create a timetable and system to measure your progress. Daily progress should be recorded. Such a move can help us know if we are on the right track or if we need to make some adjustments to our activities or plans. Measuring your progress on a daily basis will give you some level of control.

Objective prioritization: focus on a few goals at a time. Overburdening yourself should be avoided as it will minimize your chances of achieving your objective and may demotivate you. Concentrate on the important objectives first, achieve them and then you can look at addressing the others.

Working objectives into your daily plan: do something that will assist you achieve your objectives on a daily basis. The most effective way of maintaining your focus and achieving your goals is doing something that will make it happen on a daily basis. Give your objective an everyday focus, and you will have a better chance of achieving it.

A combination of such tips should be able to assist you achieve your objective effectively. Make sure you keep a progress report as it will be able to give you a measurement of what you have achieved during a particular period.

Chapter 6: Be curious all the time

There is a popular saying that states curiosity killed the cat. Contrary to popular belief, curiosity is actually helpful. It has a number of benefits that will assist an individual succeed in life. Evidence is continually emerging on the benefits and advantages of being an interested, inquisitive individual. Not only does staying wide-eyed have a number of surprising benefits, it also makes life more fun. The following are reasons why curiosity is great.

Strengthens relationships

Your social life can be made richer by your curiosity about the world and people around you. People will probably enjoy spending time with you if you can maintain many of your own interests while demonstrating an interest in what someone (or others) have to say. Ph.D.

holder Ben Dean once wrote in a University of Pennsylvania study that curious people are often thought of as good conversationalists and listeners. He further adds that curious people have a tendency of bringing novelty and fun into relationships.

Assists protecting your brain

You may have heard that crossword puzzles may assist in the prevention of Alzheimer's disease. Craving new experiences may have a similar effect. A professor at a clinic in Rochester, Minnesota, David Knopman, has stated that keeping your brain mentally stimulated is an enterprise that lasts for a lifetime. He also said that remaining intellectually stimulated and active throughout life is gaining protection against dementia.

Assists in overcoming memory loss

Nervousness can occur anytime and it is perfectly normal. For example, if you are going for a big date (maybe even the date of your life), you will definitely be anxious. Curiosity, when combined with excitement, is advantageous in that it pushes all your anxieties in the background. As a result, curiosity will enable you to effectively engage in conversation with the said date effectively. At the end of the day, you have higher chances of being successful in the date when you are curious.

Correlation with happiness

One of the many theories of happiness is that we develop the same at an early age. We are usually at this level of baseline happiness for the majority of our time. The level goes down or up depending on the negative or positive life events we experience. Our set point can be kicked up a few notches by staying curious according to Kashdan, the author of Curious? Discover the missing ingredient.

As a curious explorer, we embrace uncertainty, instead of desperately trying to control and explain our world. The end result is seeing our lives as an enjoyable quest to grow, learn and discover.

Learn virtually anything

There is a new study that was published in the journal Neuron. It found that when our curiosity is piqued it is easier to learn not so interesting' things. For example, you should take a break when you are studying and you find that you are not quite getting what you are studying about. A good option would be watching a few minutes (10 – 15) of your favorite show between study sessions. Will not only give you a nice and deserved break, but also pique your curiosity. The end result is stimulation of your brain's pleasure center.

Taking such factors in mind is proof that curiosity is beneficial in our everyday life.

Chapter 7: Leave distractions behind

How to Eliminate Distractions

Distractions are one of the main causes of failure in any endeavor. A distraction can be defined as anything that interferes with your focus on a particular goal. For example, your phone may be a distraction when you are studying and people keep texting / calling you. Though they may not cause you to stop studying, they will reduce your concentration which will in turn negatively affect your understanding. So how do you leave distractions behind?

Setting targets and thinking about goals

Thinking about your goals and setting targets for the same is the first step to getting rid of distractions. If you do not have any targets or goals, you are likely to be easily distracted. Identifying your goals and any rewards you aspire to get in the future will assist to motivate you to commit to achieving your goals. If you are studying, you should think of the grades you want to achieve and the college or job you want to get. These will be your goals. Reminding yourself of them will motivate you to reduce or ultimately eliminate any distractions.

Dealing with distractions

It can be quite challenging to deal with distractions. Some of them are your friend wants you to join him or her for coffee, the laundry needs to be done, new emails keep popping up and your mobile phone is ringing. To top it all, you may stumble across a very interesting website when doing your research or work.

When you are studying or working, you are likely to make yourself aware of distractions. If this is the case, there are some advanced strategies you can use to deal with them. For starters, the time-use diary technique is quite efficient in determining the things that really soak up your time. Once you know you distractions, you can manage them by:

· Staying focused on working or reading by thinking about solutions for the task at hand or by thinking about questions that need answers.

· Avoiding the website that distracts you. If you find yourself losing focus every time you enter a particular website, use a website-blocking application. This way, you will be reminded to go back to work or study if you get distracted.

· Increasing motivation. You will lack motivation if you feel like you are working or studying all the time. Fix times that you will use for other non-work or non-study related activities. Set an alarm for the end of each activity period as it will remind you to change mode.

· Creating time for your friends. If they are the cause of distraction, you should set a definite place and time that you will use to have a break and even go for coffee together.

· Scheduling your communication. Make sure voicemail is activated and set times when you will read and answer emails as well as return phone calls.

· Disabling the pop alert on your email. Such a move will prevent you from the temptation to read emails as they arrive. If you do not have a pop-alert system and you check them manually, try using an email blocker that will restrict access to your email for certain periods.

Such tips should effectively help you leave distractions behind.

Chapter 8: Don't give up easily

We get to the part we feel like giving up at some point in the journeys of our lives. Sometimes we give up just as we are about to realize the huge breakthrough we have been working hard to achieve. At other times, we give up even before we start. If you feel you are about to give up, don't give up! There are several reasons that will help you avoid giving up.

Anything is Possible

As long as you live, anything is possible. The only excuse for giving up is if you are dead. You have the choice of trying again and again as long as you are free, healthy and alive. You never know, perhaps the next try will be successful.

Be Realistic

Being realistic will help you reduce the chances of giving up. For example, the chances of knowing or mastering something the first time you try it is virtually impossible. Everything takes time and effort to learn. In the process, you will make mistakes. These mistakes should be used to help you succeed in the future.

Prove Yourself

No one wants to be known as a person who is weak and gives up easily. Go out there and prove yourself no only to the world, but also to yourself. Keep in mind that you CAN and WILL achieve whatever you have set out to do. Giving up is the only time you fail in your endeavors.

Has to Been Done Before?

If something has been done in the past, it means you can also do it. Even if it is only one person worldwide who achieved what you are setting out to do. The fact that they were successful should be reason enough for you not to give up.

Believe Your Dreams

Never sell yourself short. In life, there are many people who will tell you what you want to achieve is not possible while others will try to bring you down. Believe your dreams and never let anyone destroy them.

Friends and Family

The people who mean the world to you and those who you love should be a source of inspiration for perseverance and persistence. You may need to practice more, study more or even try a different angle. However, giving up should not be an option.

There Are People Who Are Worse Off

At the moment, there are people who are in a worse situation and environment than you are right now. In fact, they would be willing to trade places with you in an instant. If those people have not yet given up, why should you? For example, if you are thinking of giving up running four miles a week, you should think of the people who are not able to use their legs. They would gladly run eight miles (or more) a week if that would guarantee the use of their legs.

Giving up is not an option, but the cowardly way out. If you ever want to succeed in life, don't give up! You may rest a bit but never give up!

Chapter 9: Set up new goals

Setting new goals will always be a powerful tool in personal progress whether in your general or professional life. Goals will assist you clarify the things you want for yourself and provide you with steps that will get you there. You can increase your self-confidence by becoming more comfortable with creating new goals and working to achieve the same. The end result is leading a more fulfilling and happier life. So how do you effectively go about it?

Type of goals

Start by determining what type of new goals you are setting. Goals can be long and short term and may fall into any number of professional or personal objectives. Having different plans for all combinations that fit your life assists you become well balanced. It is even a great way to get where you would like to be.

Statement

Use a positive statement to express your goals. Stating what you do not want simply reminds you what you are lacking. Each goal should be written in complete detail including a time to complete the same. Duration may vary and may be something like the end of the day, week, month or year.

Verification

You have to verify that your new goals will meet the requirements of being timed, realistic, attainable, measurable and specific.

Priorities

Each new goal has to be assigned a priority. It will be easier to tackle if you start with number one for each set of goals, instead of all created categories as a whole. This will help you know where to start and avoid being overwhelmed.

Organization

Your resources and time should be organized in a way that best assists you succeed in meeting the new goals. It is only then that you can visualize achieving them.

Review

Periodically review your new goals and change them according to the intentions and focus of your life.

Warnings and tips

Any major goal can be broken into more manageable, smaller goals. For instance, personal goals can be broken into physical, friends or family. Professional new goals may include continuing education and career advancement. Set new goals that reflect what you truly want for yourself. Avoid using what others want for you as your goals.

Any lifetime goals should be broken into smaller increments such as ten, five and one years. You should then perform monthly goals for the year you are working on. Priorities change meaning your should have new goals. What you wanted this year may not be the same thing you are striving for in the next year. Avoid creating incompatible goals.

Once you have come up with a goal list, go back through it and ensure none are contradicting each other. Never worry too much over goals you have failed to achieve. Instead, you should use them as a lesson while appreciating the experience. The mistakes and experience should be used to ensure any new goals you set are still realistic and make sense.

These are the best tips for setting new goals and making sure you achieve them

Chapter 10: Manage your time effectively

You will be able to accomplish more each by proper time management. Applying an effective time management strategy will definitely reduce your stress. It will mean that you will be able to complete your duties / tasks on time while being more focused and relaxed. It is quite easy to become distracted at school or work. However, you can maintain a high level of productivity if you implement effective time management tips. Such tips will assist you organize your study or office time more efficiently. A few simple ides can help you achieve more in your study or work day.

Calls

Let your calls be answered by voicemail during times that you must work or study without interruption. If this is to work, you have to make sure you have set some time to return the calls you missed.

Email

You should schedule a block of time that you will use to answer email. Email, especially if you use an instant notification system, is a constant distraction. Limit the use of the email program to every three or four hours and turn off any notifications. This is better than opening and checking email when each message arrives.

To-do-list

Creating a to-do-list is very effective. Before you leave school or the office, make sure you have created such a list for the next day. Prioritize it as this will ensure you know what you are to focus on the moment you arrive at school or work the following day.

Tasks

Take not of tasks that will take no more than five minutes to complete and work on them immediately. This way, you will get rid of the small things as they are easy to forget and may have grave ramifications.

Organization

You will have to make sure your study area or office is organized. Disorganization is a major cause of unsuccessful and ineffective time management. To avoid wasting time when you are studying or working, return items you use to the locations you have assigned them, have everything on hand and keep your office and desk organized.

Prioritize

Ensure you know your priorities on both a long-term and daily basis. Make changes as new projects / assignments cross your desk and revisit your list as often as possible. The changes should also be made when other assignments / projects become less urgent or change.

Delegation

You may not need to do everything on your own. Delegate work by entrusting someone who has the time and skill to handle the same. It may be part or the whole project you may be unable to complete within the stipulated timeframe.

Technology selection

Choose technology carefully by ensuring the technology you will be using actually improves your efficiency and productivity. Sometimes, using a handwritten note may be the best method to remind yourself of a deadline or get a message to someone.

Managing your time effectively is not a difficult process. You will need to implement some or all of the above-mentioned tips to be successful in the same.

Chapter 11: Work hard, like a PRO

Tips To work Hard Like A Pro

At one point or another, you may have stumbled groggily to work on a Monday morning wishing you were somewhere else. This attitude is derived from having to work the same job day in day out. Changing the attitude is the only way you will appreciate your job and work hard at it. So how do you motivate yourself to work harder? Research and studies have shown four major methods you can use to work harder. They are:

Convince yourself you want to do the job

One of the easiest and best ways to motivate yourself to work is by thinking of the work you are about to do as being easy. There are a number of strategies you can use to achieve this. One of them is focusing on how good you will feel once you complete the task at hand. It will be a challenge for the first few times, but you will come to master the strategy with time. People who have used this method have found they have improved their performance within a month.

Take control

It is easy to be overwhelmed by various professional and personal responsibilities. One of the ways you can help yourself stay focused is by knowing that, at the very least, you can control your actions. Think about it this way; you can build or destroy the tallest buildings with your hands. How you react to situations will determine your overall performance. Positive actions will always give positive results. You should, therefore, strive to get to work early, finish your tasks on or before time and avoid wasting time as much as possible. These are just some of the steps that will ensure you work hard.

Keep the company of hardworking individuals

No man, or woman for that matter, is an island. In order to successfully pursue your goals using everything you possess, it would be prudent and helpful to surround yourself with individuals who are working hard. It may be a group of like-minded peers you meet up with after work or your co-workers. Either way, it's important to have friends or colleagues who push you to succeed. There is a saying that states an individual is the average of the five people who he / she hangs out with the most. This ultimately means you should surround yourself with hard working people.

Break your tasks to smaller tasks

Breaking up your hard work into component parts is advisable. It will not only make the tasks easier, but it will ensure you see where the obstacles are and how to overcome them quickly and efficiently. The small tasks need to be identified and handled. Any time you successfully complete one should be a moment for a little celebration. Even though small wins may seem rather trivial and incremental, they have the possibility of tremendously boosting inner work life.

Combining these four major strategies will ensure you start working hard. At the end of the day, you will be able to achieve more than you had dreamed possible.

Chapter 12: Be your own boss

How To Become Your Own Boss

Perhaps you may have wondered if you will succeed if you were your own boss. According to the SBA (Small Business Administration), the growth of the small business sector is rapid. However, a lot of people fail in business during the first two years. Even though the corporate world in America has been downsizing, there has been an increase in small business start-ups. At the same time, there has been a decline in the rate of small business failures.

The work involved in marketing, selling and even building a client base may be a large learning curve. You will have to figure out the best way to scale the moment you get things going. As much as it is exciting to start a business, it will not work for everyone. The following are four ways you can determine if you are ready to become your own boss.

You are unemployable

You may have a really great day job, but it does not mean that it motivates you to wake up excited each day. If you have always had the sentiments that you can perform better than your boss or if you experience problems finding your passion and usually shift from one job to another, chances are high that you are unemployable. Figure out what you want to come up with in life as it may be time for your small business ideas to be realized.

You prefer business planning more than your work

If you spend your lunch time lining up potential vendors and making plans means that you are getting close to making the first leap into business. It is critical to have a plan before you draft a resignation letter. Be sure you have written an effective business plan and confirmed its viability before you leave your current job. The plan should explain sales projections, include a strong marketing plan, operation details, the problems you will be solving for consumers as well as a budget that provides a roadmap for the launch of a successful venture.

You see ideas everywhere

Sometimes when you are eating out, you may find yourself strategizing on the things the owner of the establishment may do to improve the business. It is hard to turn off the entrepreneurial bug when it hits. In fact, you begin to see business opportunities and ideas at each turn. Entrepreneurship may be calling you to become your own boss if you are a person that sees solutions to everyday problems.

You have the cash

The money to start any business will have to be generated by you. Some level of startup cash is needed in every small business. You will be moving in the right direction if you have compiled your own fund for seed capital or you have been saving at least one year of monthly living expenses. Before they decide to go into business, any prospective business owner should ensure they have several clients on board. Having your first set of clients will ensure you have tested the business concept, make a few mistakes and have time to iterate before you fully invest in the same.

Chapter 13: Pay attention to details

A large number of entrepreneurs are big-picture thinkers who have a very low tolerance for details. They are very clear where their visionary journey will take them. At the same time, they may neglect the en route, practical details. We require both attention to detail and strategic thinking if we are to be successful. You may risk your chances for long term success if your big picture thinking undermines your ability to deal with details. Here are some ways you can use to help you avoid disregarding details.

Learn effective planning A great vision has the likelihood of dissipating in the confusion fog if you are unable to manage the process. Avoid such a scenario by learning how to plan all aspects of your project effectively. A good example would be getting a flow charting program. It will beneficial if you learn how to use such charts to manage the details of any project.

Take note of your cash flow Cash flow has the ability to cripple a company even if it is profitable. Never neglect this vital area of your business. One of the ways you can track your cash flow is by doing a break-even analysis as it will give you your margin of safety. It is a handy break-even calculator that can assist you figure things out.

Be courteous Everyday niceties of dealing with other people should not be affected by your focus on business. Disgruntled vendors and employees can quickly toss a wrench into your operations. Make a point to be courteous with everyone no matter how harried your day is. A famous American lawyer, Henry Clay, once stated courtesies of trivial and small character are the ones that have the deepest impact on the appreciating and grateful heart. Civility and grace make all relationships run smoothly.

Mind the small things An author known as Tom Peters suggests that people should pay attention to the small things that have the biggest impact. Peters states that there is nothing irrelevant to individual branding. Little things such as using a round table instead of using a square one to promote great flow of ideas or even changing your voice mail to be different from your competitor can have a big impact. Check all the small things in your business or company. It can be anything from the last client email you sent or the cleanliness of the bathroom to the tidiness of the reception desk. Do they indicate that you are concerned? Is each excellent?

Your communication style Having a vision and communicating it your stakeholders is quite challenging. Often, they will not be able to see what you are seeing. This is a common challenge for visionary entrepreneurs. Provide pertinent details and be specific when explaining your vision. An effort should be made to explain the ideas in concrete terms instead of theoretical or abstract terms.

Substantiate ideas by providing specific examples. Impart information using a sequential method. Make an effort and point to provide background handouts or documentation to assist others comprehend what you are talking about. Paying attention to such details will increase your chances of success in any endeavor.

Chapter 14: Make good impressions

Making A Good First Impression: Tips You Can Use

 Making a good first impression can be challenging at times. It usually takes three seconds (a quick glance) for someone to evaluate you when you are meeting for the first time. In this time, the other person will form an opinion about you based on several factors such as how you are dressed, your mannerisms, your demeanor, your body language and your appearance. The first impression is virtually impossible to change or reverse. It is, therefore, important to create a great first impression. The following are ideas that you can implement if you want to make a great impression.

Punctuality

A person you are meeting for the first time will not be interested in your excuse as to why you are late. Always plan to arrive several minutes early. Ensure you take into consideration possible delays resulting from taking a wrong turn or traffic. Arriving early is the first step in creating a good first impression.

Be yourself and at ease

If you are on the edge and uncomfortable, it will likely make the other individual feel the same way. Being confident and calm will make the other individual feel more at ease. You may take a few deep breaths to calm yourself down before you meet them.

Appropriate presentation

Physical appearance plays a major role in creating a great first impression. Since the other person will not have met you before, your appearance is usually the first thing he / she uses to evaluate you. Begin by the way you dress. What would be the appropriate dress code for the occasion or meeting? If it is a business setting, you should think of options such as blazer, suit or smart casual. For example, if your contact is in the music or advertising industry, a pinstripe suit will not strike the right note!

For social and business meetings, appropriate dress will vary with the culture and country. It is something that you should seriously consider especially when you are in an unfamiliar country or setting. Make sure you gather information on the norms and traditions.

Once you have found the appropriate dress code, grooming will be the next step. Tidy and clean appearance is recommended for most social and business occasions. Clean, tidy clothes and a good shave or haircut should be at the top of your list. For women, neat and tidy makeup is the way to go. Appropriate grooming and dressing plays a major role in creating a great first impression.

Confidence

Appearance and body language speaks much louder than words when it comes to making a first impression. Project appropriate self-assurance and confidence using body language. Greet with a firm handshake, make eye contact, smile and stand tall. All these will encourage you and the other individual feel better and at ease while helping you project confidence.

Chapter 15: Meet successful people

Brushing shoulders with success is not entirely an easy thing. Those who are lucky enough to even see the edges of the very success have a story to tell. The question remains? What have they done to get to success? Are there any risks that they have taken?

Surely, one must be willing to part with something if one is to get to the greater reward. It should be understood that in order to enjoy success, one must learn how to take big risks so that one understands the pains of making a great loss and the joy of making big profits. In this article, we will unravel the secrets that the successful people having been following.

One of the things that the successful people do is to have a work schedule. They do not just wake up on a morning and start thinking about what they will do that day. They plan for their day. Planning is a very important thing if one is to have a shot at success. This is because there is a sure way of working your goals out without the possibility of forgetting others. It makes sure that everything you have outlined is worked on because it has been designed its own time.

Successful people have goals. When we said that they work on a schedule, we did not mean that they just schedule their day without an utmost goal they aim at achieving. Remember, a man who knows where he is going knows when he gets lost, but the one who does not have the slightest idea any road takes him anywhere. What does this tell you? Successful people know where they are going. They know what they ought to achieve in a year, a month, a week or a day.

The proverbial cock crow does not find the successful people sipping from the fountain of sleep. They are early risers because they understand that time is not always on their time. They do not only wake up early, but also do it consistently. Studies suggest that the early hours provide the best conditions for the mind to work. The successful people know this and they are not ready to let it slip through their very fingers.

Successful people are always looking for new inspiration. You will find them busying themselves with newspapers in the morning, trying to find that spark that might birth a new opportunity. As a matter of fact, successful people are broad readers. What does this tell you again? Successful people are not in any way willing to let their minds stagnate.

It would do a lot of good if one borrowed a leaf from the successful people. This is because, what they do has proven so far, beyond any reasonable doubts that it is the best recipe for success. Remember, procrastination is the thief of time. You, therefore, have to rise up from your couch and start planning for your life. Map your way to success.

Chapter 16: Health

Health and Wealth are bedfellows - Go for both!

Our ancestors have an old adage the health is wealth. However, many people striving to achieve in life tend to relegate their health to the peripheries of attention. Ironically, some of them achieve whatever they wanted but lose their health. Some neglect themselves to death and what can one achieve in death? Thus, staying healthy may require a lot of effort at times. Knowing some of the ways you can use to stay healthy can motivate you and make a world of difference.

Read on to discover some of the most basic health nuggets to help you stay active and ever alert as you chase your dreams.

For the busy hard worker chasing after success, consuming healthy foods has the possibility of posing a challenge mainly because it normally takes longer to prepare. When you think of the other option, take out or eating out, you may find making a healthy meal to be quite a bother. One major key to eating healthy is making the healthy meal preparation process easy.

Achievers eat lots of vegetables

One of the effective suggestions is preparing and slicing fresh vegetables the moment you get them from the grocery store. Save them in containers or plastic bags in the refrigerator. It will be easier to quickly prepare a healthy salad in future. When cooking your meals, you should think of making double, triple and at times quadruple batches. You will then have ready lunch for the following day. Extra portions can be refrigerated for fast meals when you get hungry and do not have time to prepare a proper meal.

Make your cooking easy by using cookbooks

Invest in cookbooks that teach you how to prepare easy and quick healthy meals. Some of these specialize in cooking a meal in half an hour or less. Start by making a commitment to trying at least one recipe once a week. With time, you will discover it is quite easy to make healthy meals.

Achievers mind their pounds – Exercise!

Spending hours in the gym is not necessarily the way to ensure you have sufficient exercise. You will start finding time for exercise when you make it a priority. One suggestion would be riding a bicycle or walking to work. Of course, you need to be within a short distance for this to be effective. If this is not an option, you can use some of the many exercise videos available offline and online. Such videos can be used to exercise anytime you have some time to spare.

Some of the little ways you can use to fit in exercise are such as parking some distance from the grocery store. Taking the stairs and avoiding the elevator when you are going shopping or when in a building. When you go about your normal day, you can also do strength training exercises. For example, you can rise up on your toes while you are doing your dishes as this will exercise your calf muscles.

An achiever and water are inseparable!

Water is not only life but also begets success. When scientists list the endless benefits of water, one wishes they had a glass of water as often as possible. However, many of us forget to keep their water drinking regimen.

Since taking water rejuvenates the body and alleviates fatigue, achievers who work overtime need to take a lot of water since they are bound to often feel exhausted.

Conclusion

Staying healthy and active is not hard at all. For you to be successful in this endeavor, you will need to come up with a routine that will suit your needs. Never try to incorporate another person's routine as it may not work for you.

Bonus – Frequently asked questions (F.A.Q.)

1.   Does email have an impact on how I manage time effectively?

 Yes, it does. Schedule a block of time that you will use to answer email. Email, especially if you use an instant notification system, is a constant distraction. Limit the use of the email program to every three or four hours and turn off any notifications.

2.   What does communication have to do with paying attention to details?

 Having a vision and communicating it your stakeholders is quite challenging. Often, they will not be able to see what you are seeing. This is a common challenge for visionary entrepreneurs. Provide pertinent details and be specific when explaining your vision. An effort should be made to explain the ideas in concrete terms instead of theoretical or abstract terms.

3.   Can I use another person's routing to stay healthy?

Staying healthy and active is not hard at all. For you to be successful in this endeavor, you will need to come up with a routine that will suit your needs. Never try to incorporate another person's routine as it may not work for you.

4.   What is the most important thing to start with when setting up new goals?

Start by determining what type of new goals you are setting. Goals can be long and short term and may fall into any number of professional or personal objectives.

5.   Does punctuality play a role in creating a good first impression?

A person you are meeting for the first time will not be interested in your excuse as to why you are late. Always plan to arrive several minutes early.

6.   How does the company of hardworking people assist me work hard?

It would be prudent and helpful to surround yourself with individuals who are working hard. There is a saying that states an individual is the average of the five people who he / she hangs out with the most. This ultimately means you should surround yourself with hard working people.

7.   Does curiosity have an impact on learning boring things?

A new study that was published in the journal Neuron found that when our curiosity is piqued it is easier to learn not so interesting' things.

8.   Does giving up show you are a coward?

Yes, it does. No one wants to be known as a person who is weak and gives up easily.

9.   Is visualization important when you are focusing on your main objective?

If we are to focus on something properly, we need to have a strong visual picture of our target.

10.   Can failure to take risks be the cause of failure in a business?

In business, the majority of people who fail are those that do not take risks.

11.   Does a timeline have an impact on your success?

For you to be successful in what you want to achieve, you must work using a timeline. It is good to have a timeline in your thoughts. However, it is more effective to have the same on paper.

12.   Is intuition linked to new ideas in any way?

Listening to your intuition helps you become open to new ideas which your rational mind may not be open to.

A sincerely thank you for buying and reading this book. Check out my other books that I have on the same topic.